Light All Around Us

Light and Dark

Daniel Nunn

www.raintreepublishers.co.uk
Visit our website to find out more information about Raintree books.

To order:
☎ Phone 0845 6044371
▤ Fax +44 (0) 1865 312263
▣ Email myorders@raintreepublishers.co.uk

Customers from outside the UK please telephone +44 1865 312262

Raintree is an imprint of Capstone Global Library Limited, a company incorporated in England and Wales having its registered office at 7 Pilgrim Street, London, EC4V 6LB – Registered company number: 6695582

Edited by Dan Nunn, Rebecca Rissman, and Siân Smith
Designed by Marcus Bell
Picture research by Tracy Cummins
Production by Victoria Fitzgerald
Originated by Capstone Global Library Ltd
Printed and bound in China by South China Printing Company Ltd

ISBN 978 1 406 23813 6 (hardback)
16 15 14 13 12
10 9 8 7 6 5 4 3 2 1

British Library Cataloguing in Publication Data
Nunn, Daniel.
  Light and dark. -- (Light all around us)
  1. Light--Juvenile literature.
  I. Title II. Series
  535-dc23

Acknowledgements
The author and publisher are grateful to the following for permission to reproduce copyright material: Corbis pp.10 (© Richard Wear/Design Pics), 12 (© Randy Faris), 17 (© John Gollings/Arcaid); Getty Images pp.4 (Lars Thulin/Johnér), 5 (Reza Estakhrian), 15 (altrendo images), 18 (Tomasz Pietryszek), 19 (Sami Sarkis), 20 (Zack Seckler), 23b (Tomasz Pietryszek); istockphoto p.11 (© Neil Wysocki); Shutterstock pp.6 (© Stefanie Mohr Photography), 7 (© Losevsky Pavel), 8 (© Korionov), 9 (© Hunor Focze), 14 (© MikLav), 16 (© ER_09), 21 (© Dan Briški), 22a (© Johannes Kornelius), 22b (© Dmitriy Eremenkov), 22c (© Tatiana Popova), 23a (© MikLav), 23c (© Hunor Focze), 23d (© ER_09).

Cover photograph of light in the fog at night reproduced with permission of Corbis (Paul Souders). Back cover photograph of Earth reproduced with permission of Shutterstock (Hunor Focze).

We would like to thank David Harrison, Nancy Harris, Dee Reid, and Diana Bentley for their assistance in the preparation of this book.

Every effort has been made to contact copyright holders of material reproduced in this book. Any omissions will be rectified in subsequent printings if notice is given to the publisher.

Contents

What is light?

Light lets us see things.

Light bounces off things and passes into our eyes. This is how we can see things.

Some light comes from the Sun.

Some light is made by people.

What is darkness?

Darkness is when there is no light.

It is dark at night. This is because the Sun's light is blocked by the Earth.

It is dark in a cave. The Sun's light is blocked by the roof of the cave.

It is dark in a cupboard. The light is blocked by the doors.

duvet

It is dark under the covers. The light is blocked by the duvet.

When there is no light, you cannot see anything.

Bright lights and dim lights

Some lights are bright.

We can see clearly in bright light.

The Sun's light is very bright.

stadium

The lights at a stadium are very bright.

Some lights are dim.

Light from a candle is dim.

We cannot see clearly in dim light.

We cannot see colours clearly in dim light.

Which light is brightest?

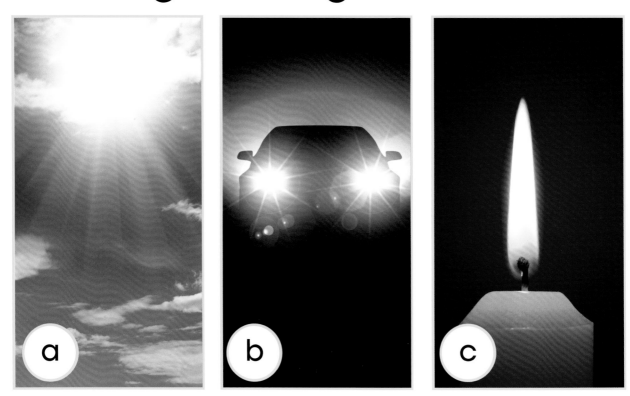

a

b

c

Which of these sources of light is the brightest?

Answer on page 24

Picture glossary

bright when there is a lot of light

dim when there is not much light

Earth the planet we live on

Sun the star closest to Earth

Index

Answer to question on page 22
The answer is **a**. The light from the Sun is the brightest.

Notes for parents and teachers

Before reading

Explain to the children that light is what lets us see things and that darkness is when there is no light. Ask them what they would need to do to make the room they are currently in dark. For example, close the curtains, turn off lights, cover any windows on doors, and so on. If possible, at the end of the discussion, make the room dark by following their suggestions.

After reading

- Ask if any of the children can remember why it is dark at night. Provide further demonstration by shining a torch on a globe, and rotating the globe. It is "night time" on the side furthest from the torch.

- Show the children a selection of sources of light of varying brightness, for example electric lights, torches, candles, and so on. Ask the children to rank them in order from dimmest to brightest. Can they see the same range of colours when things are illuminated only by a dim source of light?